Michael Oliver-Semenov was born in Ely, Cardiff but now resides in central Siberia. Since ditching his career as a banking clerk in 1997 he has published words and poetry in a plethora of magazines, anthologies and journals worldwide, including *Blown, The Morning Star, Orbis, Ten of the Best, Wales Arts Review, Mandala Review* and *Ink Sweat and Tears*. He is the author of *Sunbathing in Siberia: A Marriage of East and West in Post-Soviet Russia*. He divides his time between teaching ESL and drama to children, playing with puppets to entertain his six-month-old daughter, and drinking cups of tea.

http://thepoetmao.webs.com

T0096666

The Elephant's Foot

Michael Oliver-Semenov

PARTHIAN

Parthian, Cardigan SA43 1ED
www.parthianbooks.com
First published in 2016
© M.A. Oliver-Semenov 2016
ISBN 978-1-909844-60-5
Editor: Susie Wild
Cover design by Torben Schacht
Typeset by Elaine Sharples
Printed in EU by Pulsio SARL
Published with the financial support of the Welsh Books Council
British Library Cataloguing in Publication Data
A cataloguing record for this book is available from the British Library.

Dear reader, over the course of years it has taken to create this, my first and maybe final collection, I have at times thought of dedicating it to several people. In the beginning I thought of dedicating it to the long list of great women who have been my allies and guides throughout my life; then there were times I was tempted to dedicate it to individuals who actively encouraged me, or shamed me into trying harder and writing more often — but then that would have excluded so many great people. And so, in this, my final opportunity, moments before the deadline, I would like to dedicate this book to:

EHAHVSXIHVXEASENIEH,

QNLHMXAFXVNIXNBYQVSBX, YQBMSXET, YQBHYSVQ, HETYQFNYX.

AFSRKHRAFXNEVQKHQSPNLVTAXVVAFXKNMVT.

Contents

Distance

Birthdays are now held on Skype –
my nephew turned 14. A surprise
to see him, not as I remember
four years ago or further.

Phoning my wife at lunchtime
I smile at my daughter's cries:
a whimpering for hugs, a 'la'
at the soft animals she thinks are alive.

Christmas Day is also my mother's birthday.
No doubt we'll enjoy pixelated niceties
before screen-stare-soreness
pushes us towards a hurried goodbye.

Facebook I thee courted, wed
and father. Baby name discussions;
I love you, I miss you.
What are you up to?

Going online to talk to Mum,
Dad, sisters. To see the kids.
Lives recorded.
Never lived.

Toes

MacArthur Park always reminds me of my mother,
it was the first record she ever owned.
She doesn't know that it's on my daily playlist,
along with Enya, the theme tune to *Out Of Africa*,
and every classical song she ever loved.
Each December we'd sit and watch *A Christmas Carol*,
the musical version with Albert Finney.

We weren't talkers, we communicated through our toes
let them lock together – she would pull mine and, in later years,
my toes pulled hers. It's how we showed affection.

Before the divorce,

before my sisters went their own way,
and I went mine—
before the fighting began,
before the police visits to the 'domestic' situations
that never warranted any help—

Way before all of that: my mother was running a bath.
When it was deep enough
she pushed me in fully-clothed and I pulled her in on top.
We laughed like a mother and son do
sharing something only they know.
For once the tension didn't mute us.
I have that laugh
on my mind's mixtape, concealed,
ready to playback when our toes can no longer speak for us.

Eliot

Sitting on a rock looking out to sea,
waiting for the sun to burn through my psoriasis,
smoking cigarettes, drinking tea from a plastic cup,
I see a boy, no more than fourteen sat away from his family,
eating an ice lolly and watching the waves in the distance.
He doesn't know it but he is my doppelganger,
complete with a mop of blond hair, bowl-shaped, obviously
his mother's choice; his mother who is standing near
with his three sisters. It could have been me all those years ago;
I too know the solitude of being the only boy of four,
and remember only too well the act of sitting apart
from everyone, waiting for life to take you far and away.
'Eliot!' his mother called out to him. 'Eliot!'
before finally throwing a rock to get his attention,
which made his sisters laugh out loud.

Eliot, do not gaze too long at the ocean depths,
or the setting sun at the end of the world.
Don't let the broken bond with your mother
keep you from making a bond with yourself;
making friends with yourself is worth more than anything.

Eliot, I see by the way you lift your ice lolly to your mouth,
that you are insecure. They bully you at school don't they?
You still have not abandoned the age of innocence
when you are being seen more and more as a young man.
You do not yet know the harm that is out there,
and what it could do to you.

I watched as he left, lolly stick in hand – conscientious boy,
the bin first, mother second. He loves the world,
and has only slight knowledge of rejection.
It could crush him. It will crush him.
Eliot, not yet fourteen, if only you could know it was your
30-year-old self sat across from you, apart from everyone
waiting for life to take him far and away.

The Relationship between My Psoriasis and I is One of Love

The nodules that have settled like barnacles
on my arms and stomach are my friends.
There is nothing more blissful than catching a pustule
between a thumbnail and finger and squeezing.
Then the scabs. Oh— the tiny scabs that sequin my flesh.

How well they carpet my home.

And the scratching—
what is better than sex you ask?
Did you never pick a scab from an elbow or a knee?

Imagine your whole body an unsealable graze.

When the Guttates arrived,
friends asked if I had been set on fire.

They could not appreciate
the beauty of my constellations,

each crust of skin a falling star.

Lodger

Home is a permanent hostel where I am a welcome guest.
There is always someone who doesn't clear up after themselves.
Something leaks, or is broken, or needs repainting.
The key is yours but you're never sure about the locker.
Snoring only reminds you of other snoring, other guests,
or lovers or drunks, or times when you were all of them.
There is a shocking amount of unwanted pasta,
and most of the jars in the fridge have new ecosystems.
Found furniture creates Feng Shui disharmony
but it's only ever temporary, it'll be redecorated soon,
next month or the month after, when it's quieter;
when it's the wrong season, or when nothing's 'on'.
The shower is full of half-empty shampoo bottles,
and the lock on the toilet door is shit.
You never fully unpack, own too many socks
and there are not enough hangers in the world
to wear the different roles you play.
On the day you leave, you can't help but feel
that perhaps you stayed one day too many.

How I Remember the 1980s

In junior school we had the usual school pets –
five chubby little guinea pigs in a cage
that was passed from class to class.
They were soft, fluffy, friendly except for the
incident where Alien got bitten on the hand;
That was unusual and a bad sign seeing as Alien
could swallow worms and regurgitate them alive.

In summer someone had to take the pets home
for the holidays. My sister was chosen:
my innocent, conscientious older sister who
achieved all the As and smiley faces on her workbooks.
My mother wasn't fond of pets;
my father hated anything with more than two legs.
If it didn't speak English it wasn't welcome in the house.
To the shed they went:
all five little fluffy guinea pigs in their little cage.

Six weeks later my sister went to check on them.
It was like a scene from *Gremlins*:
a white fuzzy moss covering four carcasses;
one guinea pig had managed to survive by dining on his
    relatives.
He didn't last long enough to make it back to school.
I don't know what my mum said to the teachers
to make it right, I suppose it didn't matter.
My sister continued to get As.

Photograph

Father, I forgive you
for keeping more pictures
of your 1973, three-litre Capri
than pictures of me.

Mother, please forgive me for stealing
your family photo album,
and sending it to my father's house.
My jealousy had gone too far.

Though you may be pleased
to hear
I no longer wish
I was a car.

Memorable Firsts

I remember my first time
in the playing field opposite our house;
the local boys stood in a circle
in the far corner. I went to see
what all the fuss was about.
Curiosity led me to see a cat
– skinned, stoned, flat –
like a cartoon, only horribly real.

That was the first time I knew real fear,
watching them, their delight
their mass screams of pleasure
as each stone struck matted carcass.
The taste of death,
that acrid stench, filled my mouth,
lingered there for days.

That first time was the last I let myself
be lured by the playing field,
that dead cat would never know satisfaction,
and somehow, in that moment I knew,
neither would I.

I did learn two things from that day:

(1) No one teaches children brutality,
they know it from birth.

(2) There would come many days that
would test my faith in humanity:

that day was only the first.

For Everyone a Song

He often thinks of his past wrongs:
failed relationships, malicious
words of haste. He believes
he's made almost every mistake
a man can make.
Though life is full of surprises,
and there is plenty of time to make more.
When he recalls the worst of his doings
he hums a tune to distract his mind;
his life now has a constant soundtrack,
the bitter hum of regret.

(ii)

His step-sister has come to stay,
on weekend release from a psychiatric clinic.
There are many ways a person can self harm,
she knows nearly all of them and
she can see
by the small amount of flesh he shows
that he also knows some of those ways too well;
but they do not talk about it.
It's understood.

Instead, quietly she begins to hum,
the tune is familiar;
they hum it together.

If

And if they ask
just let them know
I've gone to watch
the river flow.

They might

want to know why

my wallet and keys
are left (inside)?

Why all I owned is left behind

and all my clothes
are still in rows?

Just let them know
I had to go,

I've gone to watch the river flow.

Shadows and Light

The moth sits under the lamp like a plectrum in a spotlight.
I am tempted to burn its wings with my lighter,
but nudge it instead, leaving gold on my finger.
It smacks the lit section of the wall repeatedly;
while I, looking over my shoulder, long
to be absorbed by the me that is indistinguishable
from nothingness.

Post-Traumatic Stress Disorder

Two nights ago my father's funeral was held,
followed two hours later by my friend's burial.
Last night I buried my unborn child;
two weeks ago my mother;
each consecutive night after, my three sisters.

Two months ago my father's funeral was held,
followed some days after by my mother's.
Afterwards I buried all of my sisters,
followed by my father again, and again.
Each funeral is held at 4am.

I have been present at my own funeral
several times, but never cried at my own passing;
such self-grieving seems impossible even in life.
Over the past ten years, four funerals a week,
making two thousand and eighty

or two thousand and eighty
one

if I count yours.

Footprints

Leading up to the court case,
those hideous days that followed your name
startled in headlines,
we tried to pinpoint the places you went;
who had seen you?
Police checked the CCTV records while
we searched, finding your handbag
somewhere near the bridge in Mynachdy.

Across the city there were traces of you
– bits here, bits there –
a rag of a recording,
a scrap of a sighting,
your jacket bottling it in the river.

Trying to locate the *you*,

before the body
laid out on the ground,

marked by a blood shadow;

handprints bruised into your throat;

size nines crushed
into your chest.

A River Runs Through It

At the backpackers alongside the river,
they are playing American football
on the large screen inside,
the sound of the game on the speakers
outside. It is night.
The main trainline is 200 yards
downriver on the right.
The bridge has lights underneath,
that change intermittently,
purple turns to blue,
blue to red.
This morning, I drank some tea here
while police divers were trawling.
Somebody
must be dead.
Everyone
who disappears in this city
ends in this river.
It's now a standing joke.
A month ago,
some 19-year-old reveller
vanished.
A friend of mine said
he'd be found in the river soon,
and true, they did
fish him out a week later.
His family taped his picture
and more flowers onto the barrier
where the Riverside Market is held.
I had breakfast there the Sunday after.

Patagoniasaurus

It never occurred to me before
that dinosaur names
were given by those who dug the bones,
or the countries where they were found.
There was a magic in them that children
never questioned. They simply were.
Like plants, insects, flowers.
Now a new, bigger titan-o-saur has been
discovered. Another planet.
My buried youth perspective is again
full of amazement;
like a newborn without tags or
national insurance numbers.
The naming process begins.
Magic is lost in familiarity. Someone
somewhere is wondering whether
we can use its image to sell burgers,
they patent the web name.
Gone are the days a three-horned beast
was a tri-something.
A two-winged flying machine
a biplane, a tyrant, a tyrannosaurus.
I wonder if, one day, my children
will question why a McNuggetosaurus
was named exactly thus.

The Building Blocks of Poetic Atheism

You say I am godless because I do not believe in the soul
yet we know animals and birds can feel: we can hear them scream.
The same is true of plants and trees; they too live and breathe.
How can you know the smallest atom is without consciousness,
when God himself is invisible in space, a nothing's mass?
When I die, no soul will fly off to stagnate in your heaven,
my flesh will be chewed and digested.
I will become soil and food for worms.
These worms will be picked off by birds,
who will fall prey to other, bigger birds.
I will become a part of everyone and everything:
the vegetables you eat will contain some part of me,
with each breath you will inhale tiny particles of my breath.

The Pyramid Effect

Jesus strolls into the market,
declares all trade immoral,
closes it down,

leaving traders become investors,
they can take your money
and return it later with interest,

Jesus, pinned atop
His mighty cross, calls up
to God and asks 'why have you forsaken me?'

Pyramids are weathered at the top
by the elements;
just as weathered
at the foot by the foot.
God is never weathered by the foot.
Neither is the investor.
Jesus however was eroded by the elements.

The investor gets on his cloud,
off to seduce another town,
while Jesus rose, and realising
He was the bottom stone
disappeared,

leaving our trader-cum-investor
robbing Peter to pay Paul,
glad of the day Jesus
shut down his market stall.

Peter goes to church
to drop his last coin in the box,
says a prayer for Jesus,
and The Holy Spirit, to get closer

to God, who has all the tickets to Heaven,
but like the investor, He can't please everyone;
He, like every man, has a business to run.
The gates will open, for some,
the rest will be forsaken.

Anthropogenic

Will they know, the species that follow, of the ones that came
    before?
Will they dig through the wreckage, create museums similar to
    those
we have with dinosaur bones?

Assuming that something comes after.
It's impossible to know when or how the end will be.

Whether it be the war I did not march against,
the nuclear reactor built with counterfeit parts,
or the telecommunications satellite that fell out of orbit
onto one of many Uranium enrichment plants
dotted around the planet.

Perhaps the next recession will bring the full collapse of society
    – the riots
become the war become the fires become the flood become the
sphere of water floating in space with 6,840,507,000 floating faces.

Whatever it may be, it will likely be entirely preventable,
in some ways I'm quite looking forward to it,
though I don't want to suffer.

Preparation is key:
I have water, the heating, the oven, my toaster
and I plan to buy plane tickets on Tuesday.
It is the job of our elected leaders to oversee us:
to ensure the groceries are grown,
that state-of-the-art nuclear facilities are erected;
that economic growth happens, that new factories are born.

Yesterday I began my day watching a video online:
the herding and clubbing to death of entire dolphin pods.
The sea ran red with blood. Now I'm doing my best to forget.

I know of the manganese ferroalloy plant being built near
    Krasnoyarsk.
I know that there is a danger during the processing of
    manganese ore,
those who live close by may see a

reduction in life expectancy, functional liver failure,
a sharp increase in cancer and the emergence of idiocy in 98%
    of all births.

I plan to raise my children there one day.

Fx

What is real and what is not real?
Primary evidence, first human witness,
though these could be tampered with,
then came video, unquestionable proof.
Yesterday perhaps, today not so.

1969 – one small step for man,
one giant leap for photography, who
would have thought when you plant a flag
on a planet with minimal atmosphere
it would blow gently
as if in an American summer breeze?

I will never visit the moon
to verify those images,
so many pictures doctored now,
most accepted without question:
John Lennon's image reanimated to sell cars
without one single public objection.

Where were you on September 11th?
I was in London for the first time,
excitedly walking down city streets,
when I overheard two men talking about
a plane landing on the Pentagon,
and wondered what abysmal new
Hollywood film they'd been to see.

I suppose it doesn't really matter.
The masses will still be entertained,
America got her war,
and perhaps John Lennon
might be posthumously
awarded Car Salesman of the Year.

Peace Crane

In an airport waiting room,
en route to New Zealand,
all the people were waiting,
all perfectly spaced,

A Japanese man sat next to
an average Joe, who became worried
he'd want to practice his English on him,
though this was not the case.

The man from Japan sat and
patiently,
systematically,
passionately
created an origami crane
only average white Joe could see.

He handed the folded paper to Joe
and explained that he was
from Hiroshima, and
at this time, every year,
people come to remember, and to learn,
from those that stayed together,
from those who burned.

The cranes are passed to strangers
in remembrance that even en route
to another place,
past horrors are remembered
and remembered with grace.

Last Orders

There are two old men that meet,

the same time every night
at the corner of my street,

to bid each other farewell
before the journey home.

I wonder why they never drink together?
Why they choose to drink alone?

Don't they long for company
now they are both retired?

Or are they both practicing
solitude,

knowing the day's not far away
when the other will expire?

The Day They Came for You

At that particular spot
Where you thought
this is the last place
it is ever going to happen,
it happened.

Then there were flowers,
although they weren't many,
the velvet rainbow of petals
appearing in the twilight hours
by the side of that tragic road.

I secretly enjoyed walking past them,
was told you had grown weak
taking hold of the side of a car
to power your bike
up the last hill of the street,
home not very far.

Your last act, be it foolish,
left a miniature Eden;
it bloomed for a week
before somebody came
to shovel up the mangled corpses.

Paramedics must have needed
the same tool,
the day they came for you.

Collected Sayings
by American Tourists

(On visiting Caerphilly Castle)

'Gosh, that castle must be like a hundred years old. Can you imagine? Everything here is just so old. It's so bizarre.'

(On visiting Cardiff Castle)

'Gosh this castle is like a hundred years old. It's so hard to imagine how they built this, I mean; they didn't have trucks then did they? It's so bizarre.'

(In London on September 11th, an hour after the twin towers had been struck)

'How could someone do this? I mean how? What were they thinking? Why? Why would anybody do this? We've never hurt anybody.'

(Outside St David's Hall on St David's Day)

'This country is so cute. You got dragons and love spoons, and even some of the road signs are in Elvish. It's just like being in the *Lord of the Rings*. I had no idea England was like this.'

40 Pence or Three for a Pound

Beneath the hanging baskets
and northern slate facades.
Beyond the peacocked gardens
and rhyming couplet bards,
many glasses broken
into many sabre shards.

Politicians deal the people
like gamblers deal the cards.
Foreign-trafficked women
fucked in midnight-crawling cars,
and the beer-bellied brain-dead
get brained in local bars.

Picture-perfect postcards
paint this city like a palace.

Beneath the gloss veneer lies
a deeper seething malice.

Scugnizzi

When we were young,
to while the time away
and escape the adult world,
we would spend whole evenings
in bus shelters.

In my day we were too few
to call a gang or group.
Intimidation wasn't our intention,
just peaceful observation
and personal reflection.

Today's bus-stop gatherers are

hunters of handbags,
thieves and thugs,
crack-smoking, knife-wielding
soldiers of the street.

To tackle this problem,
Newport County Council
has installed speakers
that play Mozart
throughout the evening—

It seems to have worked.
There are no more gangs
or hooded men lurking;
just old ladies whose buses
never seem to arrive.

Traces of Horse Meat Found in Kate Middleton's Womb

Tax cuts of £10,000, rising to as much as £100,000
will be added to
the £100bn set aside
for the replacement
of Jimmy Saville,
who is accused of
abusing his position
to buy the latest Trident Nuclear Weapons,
as a means of safeguarding the economy
from Washington
for the next three years as austerity cuts
bring prosperity to
Margaret Thatcher
who is being investigated for the molestation
of the Hillsborough Disaster;
any deterrent is useless against the likes of
David Cameron and the Conservative Party
who are under the spotlight again this month
for making record profits, though it has been confirmed
the Queen will be attending the ceremonial funeral of
the NHS, public libraries and the welfare state,
where previous sanctions failed
against democracy,
traces of which were discovered
in austerity Britain,
however the inquiry found that those
effects are more clearly seen in
North Korea.

IMMIGRUNTS

Iss the immigrunts irriz.
Don' look ut me like I'm a racialist,
theerz nuffing racist abowi',
I go' nuffing bad to say abow the blakks,
they're fine. I groo up 'wivvum'.

Iss all the uvva immigrunts wha' corziz the problumz.
Takin' our jobs. I meen, I wuldn' werk for less thun
minimum wage, pikkin froot all day, bu' sumone wuld.
Bu' they carn ge' thoze jobs cun they coz iss all polish werkers
      now inni'.

Everywhere yoo go iss all polish now, an' moozlims.
I go' nuffin agenst the British moozlims like
coz they were born ere, bu' sayin tha'
you neva know ooz gonna ave a bom on em doo yoo?

They say some of 'em cum coz iss bard like where they cum
      from
bu' woss tha' gorra do wiv us? Iss norour fault izzi'?
If iss bard over there why don' they fixxi'?
Why ave they gorra cum over yer?
Iss no' like therez no ova cuntrees to go to izzi'?

Send em back to tim-buck-too or wherever they cumz from,
thass wha' the govermunt shuld do, bu' they don't,
coz there tryin' to ge' votes in they? All the blakk votes.
I don' mind the doctuz like coz we need em don' we,
iss all the uvvaz.

Oo do they fink they are comi' to Britun?
Why azzi gorra be Britun, why no' Franss or Ostralia?
Coz they won' take um will they, thass why, they go' standards
     like.
They don' go lettin' the gates open for all-n-sundree.
You gorra ave skillz like to moov there, iss only rite inni'?

I woz finkin' ov movin' to Ostralia myself an' becummin'
won of thoze expats; burr I likes Britun, why shuld I
'ave to move coz of everywon movin' yur?
They shuld juss close the gates and start sendin' um back.

Bu' they carn cun they, coz peepl start talkin' bou' hoomun rites
     don' they.
Hoomun rites they corli'. Worra bou my hoomun rites,
thass worri wanna know? I comes from Britun and I go' less
rites than any of 'um. I paid my taksiz. I cuntributes,
Un worravi gorra sho forri'? Nuffin.
I'm tellinyoo I know we fort the natseez like bu'
they 'addi rite at the end ov the day didn' they,
I don' know much abow jooz like bu' frum worrive 'urd
they wur no betta thun worrall theez immigrunts are doin' over
     yur.

My granfarva fort in the war, iz thiss worrie fort for?
E'd be turnin' iniz grayv e'wood. E' sed this wuld appun
wen we started lerrin the blakks in, opened the flood gates
     e'said.
No' the gurkas like coz they fort for uss dinthey, still
why wuld they wanna cum yur, don't they 'ave 'omes to go to?

I go nuffin' ugainst the blakks like bu' they started I' dinthey,
if they adn't cum over then Britun wuld probubly still be
    alwhite like.
I go' nuffin ugainst the wons born in Britun coz they culdn'
    'elpi culd they.
Carn be blamed fwhere yoo wuz born c'n yoo?

Az I sed I'm norra racist, or a prejoodist, I juss wants Britun
    back
the way iwoz. Britun shuld be British shuldni'?
Peepl yoosd t'be prowd, yoosd't be a prowd cuntree Britun did
I'm tellin' yoo. Iss norrong to wanna be prowd.
I'm norra racialist, bu' therez too many immigunts an you
    knowi'.

Juss imagine wha' Britun wuld look like if none of um cum
    over.
Weed orlave jobs forra start, weed be uprowd cuntree ugen.
Yood walk down the street an evryfing wuld be alwhite like
juss like iss sposstoobe. I'm norrong am I, ave a fink abowi'.

Wen you fink of immigrunts you gorra ask won question:
worruv they ever done forrus?

I Took a Trip to the Job Centre

I took a trip to the job centre owing to the fact I had very little money, no way of making any, and like everyone else I too need a means to an end. They have these machines you can browse jobs on. You have to type in your criteria first, so I entered 'unskilled, minimum wage'. The first job that came on screen was a request for a sandwich artist. Well I can make a sandwich but whether I can make them artistically is another matter. My sandwiches have always looked appetising but not artistic. So I pressed the screen to see what the next job was. Job number two was a request for a sandwich technician. I have my maths and technology GCSEs but I wasn't sure I knew if I could apply them, I did after all only get a C in maths and the role of sandwich technician sounded rather important. I reasoned that they probably made sandwiches for NASA and the amount of salad had to be directionally proportional to the amount of meat, to be able to be consumed in zero gravity; and if the sandwiches weren't made with absolute precision we'd have astronauts spontaneously combusting in space. I did not like the idea of such responsibility so I didn't apply for that job either.

Not getting anywhere fast I decided to try applying for jobs with different criteria, so I typed in 'skilled work, maximum wage'. What came up was a request for Welsh Interior Minister for allocating funds to postgraduate scientific research projects. I remember reading in the paper about a rather expensive research project on why Cornflakes go soggy in milk in which the results were inconclusive. Now, having been out of work for some time, I had eaten many a bowl of Cornflakes and in my frustration at a very singular diet had become accustomed to watching them go soggy in milk. I reasoned that I could probably consider myself an expert in the field of soggy Cornflakes and if I were to take the role of Welsh Interior Minister for allocating funds to postgraduate scientific research projects I could allocate all the funds to myself, solving both my financial problems and the great existential soggy Cornflakes crisis. They might even award me the Nobel Prize. So I applied for the job.

I am still waiting.

Occupied Wails

Never learning your own history,
your own language
your own people,
Never quite knowing who you are.

Since when did being your own master
become a dream too far?

Anglicised.
a cirCymcision
took place at my birth
without my consent,
maybe, somewhere, my national identity
lies quiet, pickled in a jar.

I have travelled the length and breadth of Wales,
seen the people in each small village and town
struggle to raise their own.
Each coin earned, taxed to support
the opulence of the head of the occupying nation.

I'm tired of the association with our colonisers
when I leave the Youknighted Kingdom.
I'm tired of people asking how we will support ourselves
when we are our own masters again.
Economy has nothing to do with it
when you have not tasted freedom.

Are we not supposed to strive for independence
because too much time has passed?
Tell me! Is there a deadline where
the right to be free becomes egotistical ambition?

Don't get me wrong. I do not hate you.
I do not hate the English,

but my people like any other
have a right to their volition.

The Dignity of Labour

Tell me, would you really wish to be here?

Under the rain that gets through to your
very marrow, leaves you slipping and sliding in mud,
falling into skips and trenches?
Or while the sun bakes you, sweating to the point
you have to wipe your eyes every minute?

Tell me, would you really like to be in my shoes?

We make wages and only wages.
There is no spare cash, no midday coffee
in Café Verdi's. No 'Thank you for being here.'
Only, 'When will you be finished?' While the damp
drives into your bones. Shoulders freezing after
a day of digging.

Tell me, could you really live this?

In the toil and the sweat
and the pipes that carry the shit.
Have you ever wondered how it looks
after you've flushed it down the toilet?
Your quilted violet paper
looks the same as all the others.
Evidently, we are not on the same page.

When you have a go at pushing my shovel
through scalpings do you *really* feel
what the miners went through?
Has your bank account ever bled down to zero?

Stop romanticising me, your ideals
slow my steps like the mud caked to my boots.
No man chooses this life,
the cards are not dealt, they are aimed.
If it's dignity you're after, then let's trade,
you can be me, and I'll be you,
you're welcome to my dignity,
come on,
fill your boots.

Under Construction

Now I have worked on more buildings than I can count,
I can no longer recognise my previous efforts
when visiting a property decades later.
It's easy to forget the sweat and blood I have given.

Exposed and raw as a person in surgery,
I rake and smooth old joist positions, ready for the new timber.
Labourers pass me tools:
chisel, hammer, lump hammer, vacuum.

Above the joist plates, brick,
smothered in render, coated in plaster and paint.
The home owners only ever see the made-up face.
The stark reality white-washed.

These are still primitive actions.
First rate caves,
but caves nonetheless.

Few will see the bones of their homes,
or the trinkets of history they keep.
A newspaper, the cover: *Britain declares war on Germany*,
stuffed behind a skirting board.
A WW1 shirt used to fill the void above a door frame,
disintegrating like a handful of moth wings
when I attempt to unfold it.

The cigarette papers, stubs and butts of previous workmen.
Fragments of pottery.
Each and every thing a reminder that
the marks I make upon this cave are recorded.
In time my joist hanging will be scrutinised.

Future workmen will see what I have exposed.
They will ponder who I was as I have wondered
about those who came before.

There are No Problems in
the United Kingdom

There are no problems in the United Kingdom. Poor people are not demonised by the mass media, nor are they made to suffer or feel responsible for the continuing financial crisis. Members of Parliament are not overpaid and have never wasted exorbitant amounts of tax payers' money on pornography, properties in London or having their castle moats cleaned. The few MPs who were found in breach of expenses guidelines did not know they were committing fraud and therefore should not have been jailed. Those who were jailed were not scapegoats because those MPs who were not jailed committed no crime whatsoever. The British government was fairly elected and placed in a position of power by the will of the people. Big business has no influence on British politics. British banks are in no way responsible for the banking crisis which has been rightly attributed to the 'global recession' and 'benefits scroungers'. Banks do not regularly commit fraud nor employ or assign special task forces to making sure dirty money is cleaned. None of these task forces was ever called the Magnificent Seven. The particular bank that did not employ the Magnificent Seven didn't rise in status in a very short space of time due to irresponsible lending, and it could never have anticipated the resulting need to be bought out by a larger financial institution. This bank was sold at a fair price and the institution that bought it did not need a government bail out as a result. The CEO of this bank did not later become a director of the FSA. Banker's bonuses are a just reward for those who have worked the hardest. Austerity Britain is the perfect answer to the financial crisis. Middle- and working-class people do not pay the lion's share of tax. They do not feel forced into running their own community libraries for no pay because libraries are not being closed down at a rapid rate. Unemployed people are not forced into unpaid work for fear of losing their Job Seeker's Allowance. These incentives do create a greater sense of community and are there for the good of the people. Communities should celebrate the Queen's Diamond Jubilee and any Royal wedding they can get their hands on. The Queen is extremely hard working and the people should not question her expenses or her income from off-shore wind farms. The Royal family are essential to the future of the UK and understand the concerns of working-class people perfectly. The Queen's speech every Christmas Day is proof of this. Muslim people are not demonised by the media and the invasions of Iraq and Afghanistan were for the greater good. These wars had absolutely nothing to do with purposefully destabilising the East or securing a better price on black gold in any way and were perfectly legal. The War on terror is not a phrase commonly used to instil fear in people, justify invasions or to further instil the notion that more CCTV is required. The UK government is not looking to legalise the collection of data from every email and phone call in the country, and has never attempted to enforce personal biometric ID cards on its population. Britons cannot be detained without trial and no Britons have ever been detained at Guantanamo Bay. There are no legitimate reports of MI5 or MI6 being involved in extraordinary rendition cases and any British voices heard by victims during torture sessions were a figment of that person's imagination. Russia, Russian politics and Russian people are not stereotyped by the media as being corrupt. My emails, social networks accounts and medical records are perfectly secure and cannot be read or scrutinised by people in sinister locations. It is perfectly acceptable to write the name of the PM and the other guy in charge in an email, a red light will not come on in the same sinister location. They do not have the ability to pinpoint my exact location through my mobile phone or CCTV footage. The United Kingdom is nothing like the former USSR and no comparison can ever be made.

Teaching English as
a Foreign Language

To start, I am not an expat, I am an immigrant;
I do not require some special word for migrant
simply because I am born of 'the old empire'.

Please do not look at me, a native English speaker,
like I have some special kind of importance,
or relevance, or that I am to be revered.

It is I who invaded your country, you
are paying me to distort your culture,
I am the new footman of the old empire.

With every word you pronounce, with every
correction, I have you fooled, you think
I am doing you a good service.

I do not want this, and deep down I think
neither do you, but you have convinced yourself
it's something you have to do.

It isn't. If only you could see that this is
daylight robbery. I have come for your money.
Without thinking, I have corrupted your sanctuary.

We will do this over and over, me correcting
your speech, your pronunciation; I will not stop
until I hear enough of myself from you.

How much is enough, you didn't ask?
At the point you feel ready
to invade another country;

at the point you do not question
what it is you are taking away.
Then, and only then,

will I say you are fluent.

Zoo Animals

We're covering zoo animals at the kindergarten this week,
penguins, elephants, bears and the like.
As opposed to horses, sheep and cows.
Anything we don't eat.

I make my flashcards, my worksheets:
colour in the giraffe; confined to a single page of A4,
crouching slightly for want of a bigger page.
Count the penguins. The penguins confined
in a pool big enough for half my class,
and only then if they could fit in my palm.

'Don't spend too much time on it, they're only three!'
my colleague said. I knew she was right.
The rich parents dropping the kids off at 7am,
picking them up at 6pm.

'Where do they live?'
the children asked in pigeon English.
'In the zoo,' I said. 'They live in the zoo.'

The Price of Onions

I remember how you told me you live hand to mouth,
and I believed you, although you had a whole house
to keep your family in. You thought we were similar:
you doing occasional plastering jobs for some extra
cash, while the money I had was all I had.

Those sites I worked on were very often my home.
I could never picture you sleeping on insulation foam
or sofas of any kind other than your own; not knowing
the anguish of where you will rest your head is an
alien concept to those with their own bed.

Living off the Siberian land, I think of you
when I see babushkas selling berries
at the side of the road, or when I am admiring
my own crops as they grow,
knowing those vegetables need to last several
months, or maybe the year, depending on
how work goes.

The little we have is all that we have,
but somehow we make it last. I think of
you as I strip the scrags of the meat from the
deer carcass my father-in-law brought home;
I think of you lost in your concept of poverty
or as you would say: 'just making ends meet'.

Occasionally I feel what could be described as anger:
It is people exactly like you, who use all
the resources of the Earth, awarding yourself what you
think are the basics of life. My old friend,

you have no clue, but I forgive you your
self-indulgence, your petty materialism.

I would love to invite you to live off the land,
to hunt the deer. But you are busy, and I know
you would say the expense is too much,
you have to fork out for such and such,
the car needs a new something, your son
a new whatever, the next payment is due
on the thing you bought on the never never.

You will always be able to invent new sob stories
to justify your lack of charity, funny that
those who have the least to give usually give plenty.
We are nothing alike my friend, let me make that clear;
for the hungry I will cry my heart out,
for you, onion tears.

Clearing the Dacha of Snow in Early April

After driving the back way on the motorway,
when we arrive at the turning where
we are normally able to pass along
the narrow path between neighbouring
dachas, to the comfort of our own—
snow blocks the way.

The army of sweepers and shovel men,
don't come this far north; don't come to dacha territory.
For dachas are a luxury and forging paths to them
in winter does nothing for infrastructure or economy.
My father-in-law takes out three shovels and we begin.
We are now shovel men.

It's back-breaking and it takes time
to throw the snow to the side of the road
where it builds up in five-foot drifts.
We get the car to the end of the lane,
safe from passers-by;
realising it would take too much effort
to clear the rest of the way,
and we don't have the time.

My mother-in-law is first to trudge through the snow;
at our dacha she lights the stove,
starts preparing a meal of bread and cured meats.
We follow soon after, clearing the car of everything we need,
our feet sinking as they would in quicksand.

Sitting side by side we eat heartily:
kolbasa, bread, crackers,
all washed down with flasked tea and Sicouri.
We still have work to do. The water tank is empty
and needs to be filled, but we have no water.
The only solution is to fill it with snow,
if we don't, I am told our crops might fail
when we come to spend summer here.

It's an excavation of sorts, our lives measured
in ice, one layer is the storm over Christmas,
one shows early winter,
another is when my father came,
my father whose parcel of goods
arrived from Britain this morning.

With the tank full and path partially clear,
we return back to Krasnoyarsk via the same roads
that we came, only I am not the same.
My shovelling bones ache but there is something else,
a longing for home. A sorrow that comes with
the desolation of snow. It is not clear.

Self-exiled from Welsh life,
I have begun to disappear from the bottom up,
like the snow that melts from underneath,
appearing untarnished as it shrinks to nothing.
My feet are sinking and my heart aches;
is this what they call *hiraeth*?

Do Not Judge

Look at that man there, the shirtless one
in tracksuit trousers, tearing metal with his hands,
right where the children play in the evening:
that mess isn't his. He is fashioning a handle
from the broken refrigerator dumped by the park
to give to that woman stood there, exhausted.
See! The one whose shopping bag has broken;
he is taking it to her now, and refusing
the cigarette she offers in return for his kindness.
Poverty has not diminished his sense of duty to others.

See that huge mine beneath the shadow of the mountains?
Last year it was a lake. Someone in an office abroad
has claimed that land and the metals beneath the soil;
watch those sons of the gulag slave away.
They have torn down the dachas, torn down the trees,
they are tearing down their inheritance to earn just enough
to feed their families; do not judge these young men
by their rough hands or their gaunt complexion.
They would sooner cultivate the land than desecrate it,
the metal factory's fumes will put them in early graves.

Do not judge the people by the city,
they belong to the land beyond concrete,
beyond the towering residential blocks,
the crumbling balconies and the twisted metal
reaching out from the broken walkways like the hands
of the old Soviet machine buried alive.
These things are transitory:
manufactured by officials and mayors,
those who wear decorations on their chests

for want of light in their soul.
The grey men, the colourless who strive
to make the world in their likeness.

Look there! Past that electricity substation,
the one covered in military font Cyrillic code,
that babushka planting flowers in the worn patch of grass.
There in the shadow of the crumbling tower block,
her miniature garden is the soul of Siberia.

Russian Poker

Walking along the Yenisei I spied
a playing card on the ground:
Spades, but which rank? In opposing corners
was the letter 'T'. As an outsider
I wondered,
was T for queen or king?
Wasn't T also the first letter of Tovarisch?
And if this card was a comrade then weren't all
the others the same? And if all were equal
then what would be the purpose of playing?
– No winners or losers –
I left the card on the paving besides the lamp post
walked along the river, up the steps
of the monument that lead to Центральный Парк,
following the main path to the statue of Lenin.
Clearly this man held the power;
little wonder, then, that all those other gamblers
threw their hands into the wind.

The Periodic Teacup of Elements

In 2012 they said we needed water meters
these thieves with honeyed tongues.

Siberians have enjoyed unlimited water since the Soviets,
there's no need to wonder why they want to 'upgrade'.

It's the same all over Russia, what works is being
capitalised. Thirst is a profitable business.
On the news babushkas complained that their bills
were now twice, three times what they were before.
It didn't come as a surprise to me.

This week I heard they had installed meters
in our city; they are only south of the river
but it won't be long before they are here.
Today one meter was tested. Residents said
the water tasted different. They protested.
They were right, some metals were irradiated.

'An accident,' they said. 'Easily made.'
Perhaps the meters were made with waste
metal from a nuclear plant. Perhaps
everything is radioactive now.
Some of my neighbours, south of the river, are.
It won't be long before they make it this far.

00:28

I know the door is bulletproof,
– armoured, plate steel, locked –
but the slightest sound in the corridor
makes the hair on my neck stand on end.
I have seen the malleable keys available
on the black market. I try to prepare
myself for the worst; for if they should enter.
The night explosions have me on edge.
No one is able to tell me exactly why
or where they are. We ignore each
high-intensity shatter;
the cars without number plates,
their tinted windows hiding many men
who all look the same. It's not censorship
but it is by proxy. We all know what would happen
if we spoke of it openly, if we asked questions;
they would come, with their keys
that turn bulletproof doors
into paper shutters. There is no security.
We are locked in the past, thinking of a future,
where there is less not to notice.

Update from Siberia: Number 23

We have fruit flies. Where do they come from?
Thaw days are more common now
but are interrupted by days of heavy snow.
March is warm; it smells like spring, is light in the morning.
April is said to be cold; more snow coming.
The hounds of Siberia are howling
more often now and hunt in greater numbers;
they must be hungry,
I suspect they have eaten all the rats already.
I haven't seen one in days.
Summer still a million miles away
and I am out of British chocolates.

The thaw is the most dangerous time,
but the most heartening.
By day everything melts,
rivers of slush run along the pavements.
Icicles form and hang from the guttering:
it's not a good time to walk close to buildings.
The ice sculptures have been removed after
a young girl crawled inside a melted opening
and got stuck. She suffocated.
The ice absorbed her cries for help
as the search party nearby congregated.

Today is a thaw day. The sun on my face
woke me up at eight this morning.
I plan to spend the afternoon
at my mother-in-law's to do the laundry.
Our home doesn't have a washing machine yet.
I don't mind carrying my dirty linen

up the street twice a month;
it reminds me that my life so far
has been full of convenience.
Sometimes I wash my pants in the bath;
and remember how, when I was young,
my mum washed all our clothes by hand.
I never appreciated how hard she worked:
her hands red, raw, and blistered;
ice cold and yet burnt.

Moscow as Seen from Siberia

I watch Siberian eagles
from my window
as they curve and wheel
from attacking crows.
Such small birds; crows.
How quickly the eagle could escape
if it could only see itself.
A giant amongst moths.
Were it to realise its talons,
what an explosion of feathers.

The Motherland is Weeping

The Motherland is weeping!
As her musical daughters, fathers and sons
are calling out for want of freedom!
Freedom of speech and freedom of protest,
freedom to write and sing and publish!

The Motherland is weeping,
for the past has become the present, and
she can't seem to rid herself of comrade Stalin's scent!
While the sons of the gulags still slave away
for profits they never see or will ever enjoy.

The Motherland is weeping,
and I am tired of pretending, tired of
all the propaganda: the apocalypse is coming!
Tell me, if there is global destruction
just how will Siberia be the only safe haven?

The Motherland is weeping
for Pussy Riot and Khodorkovsky;
music we won't hear, words we won't read.
For all those for and against the revolution
and all those secretly fed polonium!

The Motherland is weeping
at the red walls behind the iron curtain.
Because all the sacrifice came to nothing;
for all the blood spilt and all the tears shed.
All the disappeared. All the dead.

Before Today, the Last Open Smile in Russia was in a Yevtushenko Poem

In Russia, a smile is like an invitation, for murder, or worse.
Waiting for the bus with one hand in your pocket,
like the men on the stairs of the hospital in *The Godfather*.
The curl of an end of a lip spells a break in composure:
you've let your guard down, and the men, those black-bomber-
     jacketed men
who swarm like flies to shit, will pick you off.

After a New Year's party, with vodka and all the trimmings,
we danced and sang. We smiled. The cameras flashed.
Later I receive a message: 'Those pictures you uploaded –
they show us smiling. Please remove them. People
we know might see them and think we were enjoying ourselves.'
I removed the smiles.

This afternoon I boarded a bus, city centre to suburb.
There, sat diagonally from me, was my poor Baba Luda.
How funny she looked: 70-year-old matchstick legs
in military boots heavy enough to sink her. Ticket reel in hand,
She came right up to me before recognising my face.

I thought it would be awkward. Such a proud woman,
who only ever took taxis, or begged lifts, was reduced
to such labouring: the 15-hour-day of traipsing and collecting
nineteen roubles off each and every person, on a two-door
North Korean 1950s bus that shook and rattled like a window
on its last hinge in a Siberian snowstorm.

Her face and hands creased –
laundry wrung out before it's been washed.
Her eyes shone first: the creases of so many winters
began curling upward around her eyes and mouth;
I couldn't help myself. We were disarmed
though we were not vulnerable. I carried her
smile to the supermarket and showed it to the shop assistant
who shared it with the woman standing next to her.

The Elephant's Foot

People don't realise it took seven months
and FIVE HUNDRED THOUSAND MEN.

There were innumerable deaths.

'Something has happened during the night.
A small fire, everything's alright.'

Graphite melting uranium,
buried under 1200 tonnes.

The inhabitants of Pripyat lay sleeping,
All FORTY THREE THOUSAND of them.

Relay this message to Gorbachev:
'The reactor is as safe as a samovar,
it could even be set up on the Red Square!'

Colonel Grebeniuk arrived in Pripyat
with hundreds of masked soldiers,
to find out if there was anything to worry about.
Couldn't understand why
there was a metallic taste in their mouths.

'They say Radiation has no taste.'

While children played in the street
the soldiers took the first readings:
Normal atmospheric levels are 12 millionths of a roentgen,
in the daytime the reading was 15,000 times higher than normal.
By the evening the level had shot up again.

'We didn't know the reactor was still burning.
Radiation was still spreading.'

The human body can absorb two roentgens per year.
400 roentgens is the level at which death will occur.
During that first day the inhabitants received
over fifty times what was considered a harmless dose,
they should have been warned.

The fallout would have been one hundred times greater
than the combined power
of two of the atomic bombs
dropped over Nagasaki and Hiroshima.

The Colonel had to send his men to the base of the reactor
where the levels of radiation were 2080 roentgens per hour.

'How could I send my men in there?
It would take only fifteen minutes to die.'

They went in unaware.
How many survived?

Twenty hours after the explosion,
windows should have been sealed,
iodine tablets ingested;
no such order was given,
while radiation levels were contested.

By the end of the first day, they had to evacuate.
Two hours allowance was given to pack essentials.
They thought they would be coming back,
instead they left their entire lives behind.

It took three-and-a-half hours to evacuate 43,000 people
peacefully, though with many tears and pleas.
They couldn't have known they would become
Europe's first atomic refugees.

They had been exposed to doses of radiation
that would alter their genetic composition.
Who knows how many later died of cancer?

How many of them were lethally irradiated?
There were no studies done
when the people had been redistributed.

The elderly didn't believe what was going on.
They had been lied to too many times.
One old man even decided to stay behind.

His body was found a few weeks on,
mostly bone. The rest was gone.

Forty-eight hours after the disaster, the only people who remained
were the military and the scientists,
headquartered at the Pripyat Hotel.

'These were outstanding people, specialists,
I couldn't believe they would do something so irreponsible or
    suicidal.'

There had never been a nuclear disaster on this scale before,
they thought the reactor could be restored.

Between the 26th and the 27th of April,
clouds filled with radioactive particles,

rose 1000 km above Russia,
heading both west and north.
No warning was given.

On the 28th April it arrived above Sweden,
who promptly detected a rise in radiation:
there had been a major nuclear accident somewhere,
'We had to ring around to find out where!'

A cloud of radioactive dust rained down on Stockholm.
So it was Sweden that informed Moscow.
Gorbachev had to do something.
He called on General Antochkin.

At the bottom of the reactor
12,000 tons of uranium
burned at 3000 degrees.
The fire that would bring the USSR to its knees.

The general, together with eighty helicopters and men,
went to put out the raging fire.
They flew 200 metres above
where it was an estimated 1000 roentgens per hour.

His men flew 110 sorties the first day, 300 the next.
thirty-three sorties per day, per man.
Eight bags of neutralising sand and boric acid
were thrown into the reactor each time using only their bare hands!
Five to six roentgens per sortie,
more if they were slow.
Not one of those men ever made it home.

They worked tirelessly,
before they began to throw up.
Illness was spreading, the felled men
sent off to Moscow Hospital Number 6.
suffering diarrhoea, nausea and vomiting.
Then came the latency period:
twenty-seven died quickly; the rest slowly deteriorated.

For 15 years only the first victims would be acknowledged.
The fire still raged.

30 kilometres east of the reactor, the forest was scorched by the rain.
Radioactive particles still fell over the whole of the Ukraine.
Everyone remained in the dark, only a tiny article gave scant
    information.
Those who knew wouldn't acknowledge the seriousness of the
    situation.

The May Day celebrations in Kiev were encouraged to go
    ahead;
later it become known as Ukraine's 'Parade of Death'.

It was only a week later that the
ONE HUNDRED AND THIRTY THOUSAND inhabitants
of Chernobyl and the surrounding areas were evacuated.
300,000 hectares in total had been totally devastated.

The cloud continued to pass over Europe.
Infecting Bavaria, northern Italy, France and Corsica.
It was raining cesium 137 and iodine 131.

Water pooled in the room beneath the burning reactor,
as the reactor floor became unstable;

a small amount of uranium in the water was all that was needed
for a second explosion – Minsk would have been lost – Europe
    uninhabitable.

Gorbachev had to do something.
He called again on General Antochkin.

600 men flew thirty-three missions a day
throwing eight bags of lead each time;
not one man survived.
The firemen who drained the water from underneath the reactor
showed similar courage;
their deaths were never formally acknowledged.

Some of the 2,400 tons of lead vaporised in the intense heat,
found its way into the children of Chernobyl playing in the street.

The temperature of the lead-covered reactor began to increase.
Inevitably broke the floor beneath.
Melted graphite, uranium, and lead,
pooled in the room where there had recently been water.
Below that only soil; below that an aquifer.

Once again something had to be done.
They called on the miners of the Soviet Union.

10,000 of them were bussed in from all over
to build a room beneath the reactor:
thirty metres long and thirty metres wide.
It was 50°C inside.

Masks got wet with perspiration.
Most of the men worked without them.

None made aware of the danger they were in.
Not that it would have changed anything.
2,500 died when the project was finished.
They are not in any official statistic.

Now the danger of a chain reaction was removed,
a massive clean-up operation ensued.
FIVE HUNDRED THOUSAND MEN
from the four corners of the Soviet Union
descended upon Chernobyl, Pripyat,
and the surrounding area,
their single goal, to liquidate the danger.

The liquidators: officers and generals, working
side-by-side. Rank was no longer recognised.
A sarcophagus had to be built,
170 metres long and 66 metres high.

Robots were brought in
to put the most radioactive material inside.
Only such was the level of contamination
the robots began wondering off in the wrong direction:

their circuitry melted, they went bezerk.
It was clear the plan wouldn't work.

In place of robots, there were bio-robots:
men had to tread where machinery dared not go,
on the roofs of neighbouring buildings
where the worst debris had been thrown.

Lengths of graphite, 1000 roentgens a piece.
Men could only work two to three minutes each.

The siren would ring, out the men would go,
three minutes only to shovel and throw.

Houses had to be bulldozed, entire villages removed,
The airforce sprayed everything with a kind of glue.

Who knows how much radiation everyone was exposed to?
It was later learned by those that survived
that the amount people could be exposed to
had been arbitrarily multiplied by five.

At the international conference of the Chernobyl catastrophe.
A scientist presented the facts for everyone to see:
estimating a total of 40,000 deaths.
The Western world refused to accept.

The amount of expected dead was negotiated down to only 4,000,
which wasn't made official until after the year 2000.

Still the French refute the radiation cloud passed over,
even though the rate of thyroid cancer is equal in Chernobyl
    and Corsica.

Beneath the sarcophagus stands a huge elephant's foot.
Its composition will never be fully understood;
A mixture or Corium, melted sand, concrete and 100 kg of
    plutonium,
of which it only takes a single microgram to kill one person.
There's enough there to kill 100 million.

The half-life of plutonium is 245,000 years.

The sarcophagus was only built to last for thirty.

Krasnoyarsk, January 2012

Were you early, late, or simply on time?
Maybe someone phoned you at that precise moment or
you had forgotten to tie your shoes on, perhaps
you wore new shoes that day?
Those that come with those cheap laces
that never stay tied unless you double knot them.

I wonder if you realised something was wrong?
An instinctual feeling that your conscious mind
told you to ignore; as a student of engineering
you would have been taught to rely on your
principle senses. Likely you felt nothing.

In the few remaining seconds of your life,
after the first bullet tore through your chest,
did you have time to realise what had happened?

Or did it spin you, the way they sometimes do?
Could you sense the second bullet coming?

You couldn't possibly have known that
the contract on the owner of the Lexus
you had stopped next to was due
to be fulfilled that very day
by a man who hadn't been provided
with a photograph of his target.

I wonder if he had been a professional at all.
Was it his first job? Was he in a hurry also?
Did he squeeze the trigger the instant you
came to a halt? Had you time to kneel?

Did you manage to secure your laces properly
before your life became permanently undone?

There are No Problems in Russia

There are no problems in Russia. The roads and pavements are not broken and in desperate need of repair, forcing drivers to swerve every other minute. The lowest quality of food products aren't sold here. There is no need to keep an eye on your belongings or keep a check that your wallet is still in your pocket, because there is no desperate poverty here. The militia do not take bribes, nor do they only ever seem to intervene in crimes in which there is the possibility of financial gain from blackmail. The high-rise apartments are not shoddily built, and families do not have to live in one-bedroom apartments, where the living room is converted into another bedroom every night. People do not make less than $400 a month, and their clothes are all very new and of the latest fashions. The public transport isn't comprised of old rundown vehicles from Germany and Japan, and it is rare to see a car on the road that has parts missing, or that is exhaling double the legal amount of exhaust fumes. The facilities for the people who have disabilities are more than adequate and they are not forced to live like prisoners in their apartments. The sports coach who criticised the government for lack of funding in sports facilities for those with disabilities was not sacked from his position, he retired voluntarily. The parts used to repair the local nuclear power station were not counterfeit Chinese parts bought cheap. The trial of Khodorkovsky was fair and true, and there was no political motivation for his incarceration whatsoever. The militia did not try to close down the local bookstore for housing books of political theory contrary to the democratically-voted powers already in existence, and the store was not later burned down by persons unknown. People do not shy away when you try to speak to them in the street. Journalists do not regularly disappear nor are they the victims of every one-in-five unsolved murder case. Free speech is regularly practiced. The major television stations do not show documentaries about the impending end of the world, due to climate change or nuclear disaster, claiming Russia is the safest place to be in the event, to distract people's minds from all the problems that don't exist. It is perfectly acceptable to write the name of the PM and the other person in charge in an email, a small red light will not come on somewhere sinister, and my emails, social networking accounts and personal files will not be investigated remotely. These words you are reading now are probably not simultaneously being read by official persons in an office somewhere close to where I am situated. They are probably not looking into my personal history, medical records, or trying to pinpoint my exact location. There are no regular blackouts in which large blocks of residential areas go without power for several hours at a time. These blackouts do not happen without warning. I am not listening to the voices outside the window. I am not listening to the people on the stairs. I have no reason to worry. There are no problems here, and I have not documented any.

After the Cold War

We begin seven hours apart; we are almost always seven hours
     apart,
3616 miles, and endless red tape of Russian and British
visa requirements. You take the Trans-Siberian,
on the Saturday, from Krasnoyarsk. You have no less
than four time zones to pass through before Moscow.
On the Tuesday I take the 6.30am train from Cardiff to
     London.
When I arrive, we are somewhere between five and six hours
apart, around 1700 miles and three to four times zones.
I take the 1.25pm London to Moscow, arriving at 8.30pm
Moscow time. You have already booked us a room.
There is now no distance or time to travel for us
to wake up together. The 2000 miles across Russia,
through the Ural mountains, into the far reaches
of Eastern Siberia don't feel like travelling at all. We
are motionless, a stationary train on an ever-moving
world where there is only one month before my visa expires.
We have come a long way from our first meeting in
Paris, there is an even longer way to go before
we are granted longer visas, or indefinite leave
to remain. It seems the Cold War never ended. There
are reports of spies in the Kremlin, spies in Westminster.
I cannot leave the apartment without my passport or papers.
Snow is everywhere. I remark how the difference between
London and Wales is similar to that between Moscow and
     Siberia.
People are somehow kinder here, though the poverty is greater.
The cold binds us closer together. I see a young woman
help an older woman clamber aboard an ancient bus;
watch as young men help to rake ice and snow from

an old man's small patch of garden – these harsh and
bitter conditions are no match for human kindness.
It sometimes feels like we are both trapped in Pasternak's
Doctor Zhivago, though I know in our story we will both
make it to Paris safely in the end. Thirty days pass too quickly.
It is time again to continue our journey. We take the 4.30am
flight to Moscow, enjoy one last day together. We have many
months to wait before you can hope to see a British visa.
I take the 4pm to London. When I land you are taking the
    8.30pm,
Moscow to Krasnoyarsk. At midnight I arrive in Cardiff,
While you arrive in Siberia. We are again 3616 miles and
seven hours apart. We are almost always seven hours apart.

Princess Diana Stares at Me
when I'm Trying to Sleep

During our two-year long-distance courtship, I posted my wife
500 postcards from Wales and London,
and, with the Blu-Tac I smuggled into Russia,
she tacked them all onto the walls of our kitchen and the wall
    next to our bed.
There are hundreds of Wales, one London bus, a London Taxi
    and a Diana head.

I remember the day I woke and saw the blanket news coverage
    about her death—
my mother crying although she had not shown the slightest care
    for the woman prior;
when I met a girl I liked in college a week later, saying how
    much I didn't care
about Diana made me attractive. We spent three years together.

When that relationship crashed, after a slow, undignified and
    bitter collapse,
I rented a room behind the back of the back of beyond, with a
    view to die for.
Inside the boiler cupboard in my room, my landlady kept boxes
    of her twenties,
where she also stashed the obligatory Diana biography.

My mother even kept a newspaper with Diana's death holding
    the front page.
Years later a dinner plate appeared. On Sunday afternoons we
    would cut
the chicken only to find the people's princess – animal
juices and pieces of meat bleeding all over her wedding dress.

It's become the 'Where were you on the day?' for my
    generation.
Can you remember the day before or the one after?
I have been affected by many car accidents.
I have seen a young girl stand
after a motorcycle joyrider had taken off her leg—
the limb left dangling and twisting by a thread of skin.

I have seen a careful motorcyclist, covered in reflective gear,
knocked down dead by a silver Mercedes Benz in rush hour.
Still, none of these compare to my mother's accident.
Policemen brought her banana-shaped post van to our house.

She came home, eventually,
and though she could walk then, she cannot now.
The Tories are trying to knock her disability payments down.
Her fight against hunger and homelessness,
her own car accident, eclipsed by a stranger.

Why do we measure our lives by pre- and post- the people's
    princess?
I sent a cardboard cut-out bust of Diana to my future, coupled
    self,
but without that card, it would be one more day I couldn't
    remember.
Date-stamped, I can tell you exactly when and where I was,
like the day we lost Diana.

I don't even know the year I almost lost my mother.

In Your Wake

You leave before my eyes open,
return just after I've left.
When I'm home in the evening
you work your night shift.

We are much less passing ships in the night,
more, boats in different corners of the same ocean.
You have left me some pie in the oven;
made the bed and put the washing on.

A thicker cover has been laid over the duvet;
the unruffled sheets make me pause;
before I fall asleep I switch pillows,
and bury my face in yours.

We know each other only by the signs we leave behind.
The clothes in the wash basket, a trace of your scent.
Each hoping for a glimpse of the other
through the streams of our displacement.

While You're Sleeping

I don't like to sleep when you're not here,
preferring to play computer games,
read, and update Facebook too many times.
I smoke more cigarettes than is good for me,
if it can be said any of them are.

I drink tea on the balcony, watching
the evening strollers five floors below
making their way home, with shopping
or coaxing children, or dogs; and the night people,
the ones who piss against the electricity substation
thinking they are out of view.

My weary eyes double-take everything as three
turns to four; and four to five. I write this, and that
but nothing of any worth. It's all to keep me
awake. I think of you sleeping
hunched over, in your chair by the desk.
Occasional bleeps preventing any proper rest.

And phone calls. Those late night calls
from engineers repairing things that nobody
will need until tomorrow morning.

I think of you sleeping soundly,
next to me on the bed, snoring like a herd
of bears, on a train, in a jungle.
You'd think I'd use these quiet nights to rest,
but that infuriating jungle comforts me
somehow. Even the way you wriggle into
the middle of the bed
spread like a star,
with child-like limbs everywhere.

Hedgehog

A former lover nicknamed me Hedgehog,
something to do with my spiked hair,
my apparent slowness.

How many times have friends asked me
– 'If you were an animal which one would you be?' –
unable to see which creature I was like?

How did she get it so exactly right?

Though I don't think she knew of
my constant longing for hibernation
or how many times
I had come close to casually walking
in front of a moving car at first light.

How Many Harlequins?

At the beginning of our affair
she led me to her apartment,
the one I later learned
had been borrowed from a friend.

Pointing at the wall,
specifically, a print of
Guernica, she asked
'How many harlequins can you see?'
Confident her knowledge of art
was greater than mine.

To avoid revealing my ignorance
I remained mute,
turning instead to admire
the masterpiece of her eyes:
not seeing a single harlequin
when I should have seen many.

Magpies

'I always see them alone,' I said.
'Never two at once.'
'When you see one on the ground,
the other is never far away,' she said.
'It is usually in a tree.'
We watched as one flew
to join its mate,
the sag of branch.

I thought of this, years after
she had left me for another man.
Her PhD over,
opportunity calling her elsewhere.
She flew away, back to
where the other man had been waiting
like a magpie in a tree.

Two will never bring me joy.
Never three for a girl, four for a boy.

On Days Like These

My Natasha PhD bred trays of flowers to counter disease.
Had me on my knees collecting hair clips from under her bed
in the apartment she had slept in, just after she had left me
bereft of anything resembling joy, which since
I have another's hair clip now, I am willing to forgive.
Our chance encounter came in-between her tango classes
but for all the flowers she bore, left me only a cactus
and a tomato plant at my front door, where we met
for the last time, after I had promised not to see her.
And so we walked to the station for the last time
knowing I would wither, and she would be fine;
her olive skin reminded me of the plants she grew;
she was nature, flowers, disease, everything at once.
Those afternoons we spent making love
to Einaudi. The time she blushed
when we went to the shop for only condoms and a toothbrush;
the time I left her naked so I could buy more protection, finding
her, an hour and several shops later, in the same floored position.
What could be said if it weren't for nostalgia?
Her name was Natasha and she danced the Taranta.

How I Feel Knowing the Kind of Pornography You Watch

In your most intimate moments alone
it is not my face you picture.
So do you see me when we are alone together?
You don't, I know; eyes always closed.
I'm supposed to say that it's alright,
it's perfectly normal and I don't care.

But you should know that I have come to crave
a solitude so deep, that even I am not there.

The Woman with Puppet Hands

No one ever talks of the last moments of those accused of
    witchery.
Who knows how many went mad or
threw themselves into the river beforehand,
as a means of defiance. For what would await you?
Mouths open in faces you knew,
too afraid to protest your innocence;
a mob, rabid with accusation;
frothing with nationalism.

Romance is Dead
Long Live Romance

Sitting opposite you in a café, I notice how
the skin on your arm is sagging by the elbow.
The long hairs above your lip have grown
into a moustache I love but can never mention.

Do not be embarrassed. In twenty years time,
even if you have a beard longer than mine
and your skin hangs looser, I hope that we are still
sat opposite each other, so that I can look at you.

You Asked Me

You never looked more beautiful than when you were in the
  shower.
Wrapping both your arms around your pregnant belly:
'Don't look at me, don't look at me.'
I refused, closing the door behind me.

You asked me why I loved you and my mouth froze,
though if I had answered I would have said this:
'It is your awkward smile, the way your lip curls upwards
only on the right side of your mouth, your accidentally sloping
  fringe.
It is the unfeasibly long eyelash on your left eye,
which growth-spurts while all the others remain slow,
as you like to appear to be.
It is your lack of direction and your clear sense of purpose;
when even in doubt you always seem certain.

It is your gelfling-puppet-hands and your elvish hair,
your elvish hands and your puppet stare,
and the way you look at me, surprised and embarrassed,

using your hands to cover your cesarean scar,
which, by the way, is proof my school teacher was wrong
when she said
there are no straight lines in art.

When I Return Home, I Begin Mourning Again

It is not that you are somewhere else
somewhere I do not know,
I am not so fickle or possessive. I am happy
so long as you are living and free.
It is the mark upon the pillow;
the knowledge that the air I breathe,
was once shared – so
I gulp it up and resent
anyone else who fills their lungs with
us, as we were, when you were here,
before I returned home, and began
mourning again.

Be with Me Now

I am surrounded by what should have been inspiration:
a distant wooden hut under a willow, dragonflies dodging
flowers I don't know the name of in any language;
sycamore helicopters bookmarking my pages.
Children play at my feet, softening the consonants
of words whose meaning can only be understood
if you are two and the swimming pool is an ocean.
Yes, when the sun shone and the wind and the nowness
of everything was what should have filled page after page,
I couldn't write the poem that was meant for you. But,
if you should find a brief moment between this and that,
and words exchanged in-between have-to-be-taken-care-ofs;
you'll find my poem in the rings inside your coffee cup;
in the mark left by your lips; in the seconds where you
paused long enough to hear everything I left unspoken.

Ghosts

Your image moves in sepia everywhere you were;
always when I'm home you are in the shower.
I ignore your pleas to help you with the tap
only to find you in the kitchen, knees to chest
demanding tea. Turning from you I go to bed
only to find you there also, naked and glorious.

If the spoons could talk they would speak to me
of how you held them. The bed would call your name
and the hooks would mourn the absence of your coat.
The shower head cries incessantly, knowing
it will never again taste the water that soothed you.

You are always in a hurry to get dressed and head
for the places you know where the opposite is true:
rooms that have never known the you as only I know;
a sacred place that saves you from the torment
of seeing the ghost of you repeatedly come and go.

Something Resembling Resentment

In an infinitude of scheduled parties,
excitements and have-to-be-seen-ats;
the time that was the last pink cloud
over the highest of the highest peaks;
the deepest of the blues and greenest
trees; the lions and the tigers, mythical
beasts; first parental book readings;
everything seen and unseen; coffee
on the Champs-Élysées; and, and,
I want to hold your hand and say
that the word 'I' will now be erased
from my vocabulary; that 'my'
and 'mine' are now 'you' and
'yours.' But you don't hear me.
Your phone keeps ringing and
it's clear you're itching to be
where the caller is, where it's cool
to be seen at; because dreams are
for dreamers, and there'll be more
pink clouds some time in future.

Butterfly / бабочка

Not fully-formed, you are lying inside your mother
in the exact same spot we made you to keep warm;
the heating was off at the time, as was the water,
neither of us knew we were creating a daughter.

Those shadows you see moving in a circular motion
are the hands you will hold halfway through life;
they are big and strong enough to eclipse the light.

You kick when something sounds or smells wrong
and dance when there aren't any songs playing;
things I wouldn't have been good at teaching.

And with those two most valuable lessons learned
I have but a few things left to tell you.

First: do not look to me
for all the answers because I have none;
and second, though by simple relation you will know me
as your father, see me instead as a butterfly farmer,
whose only dream is to marvel
at the colour of your wings
before you fly free.

I Want to be There

Where time and space do not allow.
In your photograph, where then and
now is the difference in a day's age.
Where you were, who you were with,
to both watch and be your first kiss,
first caress; to collect every tear you
have ever shed, and be everyone
with whom you have ever shared
a bed, a hug, a glance, an exchange
of moments, pains, achievements,
careers and family engagements.
To be there, where you are, now,
and forever, and count every blink
of your eyes, an infinite number of
butterfly wing closures, slow-motion
flutters; to see you first born without
a trace of life's tensions, or a care;
your last living moments; everything
in-between. I want to be there.

Acknowledgements

Acknowledgements are due to the publishers and editors of the following magazines and anthologies, in which earlier forms of some of these poems first appeared – *Nu Fiction and Stuff*; *Blown Magazine*; *Dear Sir*; *Ten of the Best*; *Nu2 Memorable Firsts*; *Cheval*; *Poems for a Welsh Republic* (Red Poets Society); *Lampeter Review*; *Red Poets Magazine*; *Orbis*; *The Morning Star*; *Mandala Journal*; *Ink Sweat and Tears*; *The Stockholm Review of Literature*; *L'Atelier d'ecriture*.

Also, BBC Radio Wales; BBC Radio 4; and TVK Krasnoyarsk.

Author's note: The majority of facts in the poem 'The Elephant's Foot' were taken from *The Battle of Chernobyl* (© **M Way Films / Discovery Communications Inc / Corbis Sygma – 2006**), a documentary film written and directed by Thomas Johnson.

Thanks are due to the following people who helped in significant ways or were especially supportive: Aida Birch; Amanda Birch; Jean Perry; Alan Perry; everyone at the Terry Hetherington Awards; Mike Jenkins; Jonathan Edwards; Hugh Lester; Dominic Williams; Dougal, for the sofa, not killing me, the carpet in the kitchen, the sleeping bag, and all of the Riccy Toasty Specials or whatever the fuck they were; Emma Geliot; Rachel Trezise-Frowen; Mab Jones; Mark Blayney; Ailbhe Darcy; Philip Nikolayev; Tiffany Atkinson; Rhian Edwards; Natasha Spadafora; Richard Marggraf Turley; Katie Evans-Bush; Zoe Brigley Thompson for being so wonderful, going beyond the call of long-distance friendship and showing me how; my family in Wales, Lindsey especially; Horatio Clare for telling me every poem of mine you read was great even when it wasn't, for the wine, and the wise words in the late hours, with wine; Ray Edgar for all the support, encouragement, and general kindness when you could or should have acted otherwise; Dannie Abse, for always being so lovely and the letter I never expected to receive; everyone who gave me a place to sleep when I had none – there are too many of you to count and some of you I only met once; the staff at Oystermouth Library, Canton Library, Cardiff Central Library, Swansea Library, and Llantwit Major Library.

Extra special thanks are due to Natalie Konno for all the things you have given me in place of THAT mint ice-cream, making fun of me often, and reintroducing me to a world I thought lost.

Extra doupleplus special thanks are due to my wife for putting up with me every day, being a human compass, an excellent mother, and leaving alone any future chocolates I choose to hide in the cupboard above the kitchen door.

Super extra doupleplus special thanks are due to the unlikely couple: my editor and comrade, Susie Wild; and my cover designer and comrade, Torben Schacht. You have both given me more than I can ever hope to deserve and I wish you every happiness.

PARTHIAN

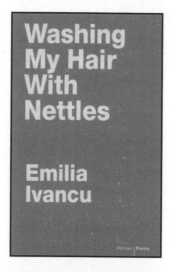

Washing My Hair With Nettles

Emilia Ivancu

Parthian | Poetry

Tattoo on Crow Street

Kate Noakes

Parthian | Poetry

Living in the Delta

new & collected poems

Landeg White

Book of SONGS

POETRY

PARTHIAN

www.parthianbooks.com